FRANK WOOTTON
50 YEARS OF AVIATION ART

TYPHOONS TAKING OFF
FROM A NORMANDY AIRSTRIP 1944

FRANK WOOTTON
50 YEARS OF AVIATION ART

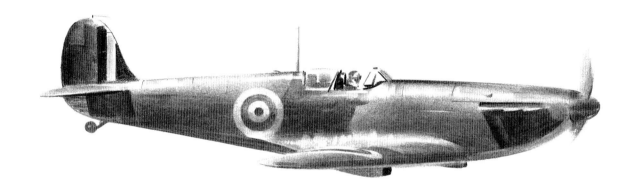

David & Charles

British Library Cataloguing-in-Publication Data

Wootton, Frank
  50 years of aviation art by Frank Wootton.
  I. Title
  758.092

  ISBN 0–7153–9874–1

Typeset by ABM Typographics Limited Hull
and printed in Singapore
by CS Graphics Pte Ltd
for David & Charles
Brunel House   Newton Abbot   Devon

CONTENTS

FOREWORD

THERE HAVE BEEN a number of books published which have either concentrated solely on the aviation paintings of Frank Wootton or have included them in a wider review. Now, at last, the great man himself has produced his own book about his aviation paintings. Reviewers of earlier books, both British and American, have been lavish in their praise of his work. The greatest American tribute has been an exhibition of his paintings in the National Air and Space Museum of the Smithsonian Institution in Washington DC.

As an aviator myself I have always taken a keen interest in paintings of aircraft and of aviation scenes generally. Sadly so many such paintings do not leave one with the impression that the aircraft could actually fly; in addition, the skies seem unreal. Happily, however, there are a few artists, and to my mind Frank Wootton is outstanding amongst them, who produce magnificent living scenes and the viewer can genuinely feel airborne.

Whilst I have always admired Frank's paintings since he was an official war artist in Normandy and Burma during World War II, I did not meet him until 1970. At the time I was commanding the Far East Air Force with my headquarters in Singapore, and the Air Force Board decided to place on record the activities of the Far East Air Force before it was disbanded towards the end of 1971. Frank Wootton agreed to undertake the task and whilst doing so, based himself in my house in Singapore. My wife and I were delighted, because we both take a great interest in paintings and had always wanted to meet Frank. In addition, it would enable us

to see and learn more of his remarkable work.

On our return to England I found that Frank was a near neighbour in Sussex. We have become close friends and my experience and knowledge of his painting has increased considerably, as has my admiration for his work. I retired from the Royal Air Force over fifteen years ago and I find Frank's paintings very nostalgic. They cover such a wide span in the history of aviation, civil and military. One of his particular

skills is to research some noteworthy action involving aircraft and then to compose a remarkably accurate picture of the event. There are two good examples in the book: first, there is his realistic picture of SE5A aircraft during World War I (page 34), and, second, his excellent reconstruction of the siege of Habbaniya in Iraq during World War II in 1941 (page 51).

Frank takes great trouble in his search for technical and historical accuracy, covering not only the technical aspects of the aircraft involved but also the background to his composition. He has a gift for presenting an aircraft in a manner which shows it to advantage as something of aerodynamic beauty that really does fly. When you add to that an ability to reproduce natural and beautiful skies for a backdrop, it is not difficult to appreciate why those of us who fly admire his aviation paintings so much. Naturally, Frank is himself keen on flying and a number of his remarkable pictures illustrating an airman's viewpoint are the result of many flights as a passenger. This is particularly true of the painting of a pilot's view approaching the runway at Gan in the Maldive Islands (page 87) – a view I have often had myself.

I am delighted that Frank has now produced this comprehensive book of his aviation paintings. His contribution to the history of aviation is immense, for which the flying world will always be grateful.

It comes as no surprise that he was for many years the President of the Guild of Aviation Artists.

Air Chief Marshal Sir Neil Wheeler
GCB, CBE, DSO, DFC, AFC

EARLY WAR YEARS

SUNDAY 3 SEPTEMBER 1939 was a brilliant sunny day. I had just finished mowing the lawn when Mr Chamberlain's fateful broadcast announced that we were at war. The following morning, after completing unfinished work and writing a number of letters to all who may have been concerned, I reported to the nearest RAF Recruitment Centre in Brighton. I came away feeling impatient and depressed with the prospect of having to await my call to service and the sluggish response to my application to serve in the Royal Air Force, although it was not long before I received a buff envelope from the Air Ministry.

To my surprise, it contained not an invitation to join the service, but to visit various RAF stations to record the work of the Royal Canadian Air Force. I understood that I would be usefully employed during the period between attestation and the time when I would be called up for active service. I presented myself at the Air Ministry where I met the Director of Public Relations, Air Commodore Harold Peake. He knew of my work and the interest I had in painting aviation; a number of my paintings had found their way into the various command headquarters. Air Commodore Peake was the first commanding officer of No 609 West Riding Squadron in 1936. He explained to me that Canada had sent over two of its squadrons together with their aircraft to assist Britain in the war. He wanted me to record some of the work they were doing. The first squadron was No 400 RCAF, based at Odiham, the second No 401, at Digby.

I started work immediately and was greatly impressed by the high-spirited enthusiasm I met on my recep-

tion. I found the Canadians of all ranks congenial and relaxed and very understanding of the work I had come to do. Without any formalities, they flew me wherever I wished and collaborated with incredible patience. My reception at Digby in Lincolnshire was equally enthusiastic. The squadron was No 1 Squadron in Canada and had adopted the prefix of 400 to avoid confusion with the British squadrons. Their air-

Wing Commander Gordon McGregor, 401 Sqdn, RCAF. *With acknowledgement to the National Aviation Museum of Canada, Ottawa.*

craft were Hurricanes, led by Squadron Leader McGregor, who had a distinguished record of fighting. On one occasion, the squadron had achieved a tactical victory, breaking up a defensive circle of German Me110s. The Me110 had forward-firing and rear-mounted guns, and when flying in a defensive circle any attacking aircraft was most vulnerable. Squadron Leader McGregor explained that they had planned the attack with great precision, working out the firing angle of the guns fore and aft. The interception was plotted and carried out with the calculated angle of attack and the enemy formation broken up with the loss of two enemy aircraft and others damaged with no loss to No 401 Squadron.

NORMANDY, 1944

I AM NOT LIKELY to forget that summer afternoon in June 1944 when the Commander-in-Chief Allied Air Forces, Sir Trafford Leigh-Mallory, asked me if I would like to paint the work of the Royal Air Force at war in France. His second question was, 'How long will you need to collect your painting equipment?' My answer was: 'Two days'.

On my return to Supreme Headquarters Allied Expeditionary Air Force there was an Avro Anson at Northolt ready to fly me to Normandy. I was driven to Northolt by Group Captain Urmston, Chief of Intelligence, who had assisted me with some new additions to my uniform as a Special Duty Officer. As we approached the aircraft, an army captain and a brigadier, who had been in conversation with the pilot and navigator, came across and asked the group captain if he would allow them to accompany me. I was not prepared for the group captain's reply, which in effect was

that as the aircraft was specially commissioned to take me over, the request should be directed to me. We were flying to a forward airstrip, but the pilot assured us that he could take the army officers to their destination en route. The group captain thought he would like to join us, just to set foot in France, although he was not allowed to stay. This was the first of a long series of flights I was to make as an official war artist to the Royal Air Force.

By the time I had wound up the undercarriage we could see the Channel. The French coast was visible from afar, the sea darkened as far as the eye could see by a fantastic mass of ships. Altering course slightly, the Anson lost height, and with lowered gear landed in a thick cloud of dust on an airstrip. An army jeep drew alongside and we waved goodbye to the brigadier and his captain. We taxied to the end of the strip, turned round and took off for our own destina-

tion. The pilot said there was no time to wind up the undercarriage and, with a steep banking turn, we landed once again. When the dust had drifted away, an airman appeared and escorted us to a caravan. It belonged to Colonel Preston, whom the group captain and I had met when he was Secretary of the Royal Aero Club. We stayed briefly for a welcome drink in his caravan and a quick explanation of the purpose of my visit. Colonel Preston gave us a clear picture of our position in relation to other sites and pointed out on a

map the construction of other airstrips in progress. One of his guns defending the strip, a mobile Bofors manned by the Royal Air Force Regiment, had brought down the first Me109 during the landings and, moreover, with an economical two rounds. I made a quick painting of the gun and its team. The subject being stationary, this was a good exercise to check my materials in unfavourable conditions. Several years afterwards I saw the painting once again at the Air Ministry in London.

The bridge-head was small and the beaches congested, everyone busily engaged in their own sections. I sought the best unit I could find to obtain an overall view of the operations with a daily update of movements. No 35 (Recce) Wing had just arrived on 22 July at Beny-sur-Mer (B3). Previously the Wing had been based at Gatwick under the command of Group Captain Peter Donkin.

On 6 June, in the early hours of the morning, No 2 and No 268 Squadron had taken off from Gatwick for the Royal Naval Air Station at Lee-on-Solent. The air liaison officer was Captain Jim Palmer with No 268 Squadron which was commanded by Squadron Leader Bert Mann. The two squadrons had been engaged in spotting for the naval bombardment of the German coastal defences. The ships, all cruisers, directed by No 35 Wing, were HMS *Belfast, Hawkins, Kempenfelt* and *Mountcalm.* The initial landings were reported back to the Royal Navy at the request of HMS *Glasgow* in order to lift the bombardment from the first targets on the beaches to the secondary targets further from the shore, and thereby ensure that there was no accidental shelling of our own forces. The group captain, Peter Donkin, insisted on flying a sortie. Following the spotting task, the pilots were briefed on purely reconnaissance missions. Two pilots from No 268 Squadron were the first to land in France in order to refuel. The first landing strip was, I believe, constructed within forty-eight hours of the initial landings, by airfield construction units. This was easily achieved by bulldozing the sandy soil and laying the interlocking steel sheets which formed the runway and taxi paths to

dispersal points. Whilst these strips were being prepared, the airfield was still under sporadic fire from both the odd sniper and enemy artillery.

On about 22 July, having been moved from Gatwick to Odiham, No 2 Squadron was preparing to move once again, but this time to Normandy. Half-a-dozen Dakotas carried the ground staff, whilst the mobile operations room and various other trailers went by sea from Gosport. No 2 Squadron was already operating from B3 at Beny-sur-Mer before the seagoing convoy had embarked. No 268 Squadron followed, reporting to the newly erected intelligence operations set-up, to which I made my way and reported. Sir Trafford Leigh-Mallory had granted me complete freedom of movement, which I carried in the form of a letter signed by him. This also requested the use of any form of transport wherever I wanted to go.

I was fortunate to meet many good friends on this

Wing. Squadron Leader Laurence Irving, senior intelligence officer, who by a happy coincidence knew my work, immediately made me feel at home. Being an artist himself, he knew exactly what I would be wanting to do. I was taken into the briefing room and introduced to Peter Donkin, the group captain, the squadron commanders, pilots and the army liaison officer, Captain Jim Palmer. It was here that I found what I was looking for, a complete information centre receiving instructions from the army and the air force, photographing the German resistance daily, both from high altitude and low-level flights. The photographs were processed by the squadron photographic sections, from which the army liaison officers and the RAF intelligence officers were able to do first phase interpretation from wet prints eight minutes after the landing of the aircraft. Officially, no offensive action was taken by Nos 2 and 268 Squadrons, but whilst

it was frowned upon, more often than not it was accepted. It was the recce results that were the priority, while the pilots could, and often did, call up and initiate attacks by Typhoons.

While I was being driven around to meet the various squadrons and pilots, Peter Donkin drew my attention to the airstrip which was crowded with airmen and pilots anxiously awaiting an incoming aircraft. It was one of No 4 Squadron's Spitfires carrying a forty-five gallon drop tank. The men were anxiously awaiting its arrival and to see it safely down. An irregular 'regular' run had been arranged from England to France. Appa-

rently Malcolm Barclay, the army G2 had some influence with a brewing firm who filled the drop tanks in England.

My first night in France was a memorable one. I had, by a happy coincidence, found space in a tent occupied by a Canadian PRO whom I had met in England. I laid my groundsheet down and, with my greatcoat for a pillow, soon fell asleep. I was rudely awoken by the Canadian, clad in pyjamas and tin hat firmly strapped under his chin, shaking me and demanding that I get up and put my own hat on. Thanking him for his concern, I asked what was going on, to which he replied that we were being strafed by low-flying aircraft. I enquired whether we had a foxhole or slit trench nearby, to which his answer was in the negative, so I crawled back into my bed saying that I thought he was offering the Luftwaffe a better target prancing around the tent than I did lying down. I must have been extremely tired, for the next day I learned that not only had we been shot up by low-flying aircraft but also shelled by a long-range gun, which had our range. Aircraft were sent out the following day to search for the source of this nuisance. Unfortunately, it could not be located and each night we were subjected to long-range shelling. Then someone suggested a night search when the flash would reveal its position. By careful timing and navigation it was pinpointed. The gun was located near Pont l'Évêque in a disused railway tunnel, retreating therein during the day and only emerging at night. The next day we buried it, for two Typhoons were sent out and closed both ends of the tunnel; with extra guns on the airfield, our nights from then on were relatively peaceful.

The Typhoons of No 83 Group, which first operated from the beach-head, had developed inexplicable faults, largely due to the abrasion of the sleeve valves from dust, which was increasingly prevalent. It was all-pervading and choked everything, permeating the tents and coating the entire beach-head. A geologist pointed out that Calvados provided the crushed grit used for the manufacture of emery paper. Filters were employed for the Napier Sabres, while the concen-

trated use of so many aircraft and the quickening tempo of operations using so few strips aggravated the situation. Water sprayed on to the airfield after dark minimised the trouble.

There was a diverting moment when, the following morning the senior intelligence officer called me over to his caravan and showed me a copy of *The Times* of that day which had been flown out with the mail. Laurence asked me to look at the back page on which was illustrated the mural I had designed for the newly-built de Havilland workers' canteen at Leavesden. It is a source of wonder that in the midst of this tactical administration of the great landing and tremendous supply problems the mail should be arriving at a speedier rate than forty-five years later. The mural was of special interest to me as I had designed it to be carried out by students, since it was not feasible for me to do it myself. It consisted of a number of large photographs taken by Dixon Scott, whose work often appeared in *The Times*. He sent me a selection of country scenes, such as ploughing, sowing, harvesting. These were greatly enlarged and mounted on boards about an inch thick. The edges were vignetted to make coherent shapes. They were in black-and-white. When mounted on the walls, the students painted from my designs the walls between the photographs with incidental figures and animals relating to the photographs. Apparently it worked very well, the only mishap occurring to one outsize photograph which, when mounted on its support, proved too large to go through the doorway. A workman had solved the problem in his own practical way by sawing it in half.

HORSA GLIDERS

S OME WEEKS LATER I drove down to Ranville to see the results of 'Operation Mallard' and the glider landing fields. Pegasus Bridge was intact and Staff Sergeant Wallwork's glider beautifully placed remarkably close to the bridge itself in a perfect position for the assault. All three gliders had been flown with great precision, casting off at 500ft over the coast three-and-a-half miles from their landing zone. I learned that Air Chief Marshal Leigh-Mallory remarked on this brilliant feat of airmanship.

East of the River Orne were 246 Horsa gliders of the 6th Airborne Division, and they were holding the left flank of the 21st Army Group. I was impressed at the landings, seeing no collisions. Moreover, the gliders were evenly distributed over the area as if to plan. It was a scene that would have delighted any surrealist painter, an incredible disarray of grounded aircraft, wing tips on the scored grass and the others slanting to the sky, tails blown off by charges for easy exit of the troops. I sat on a discarded tail and started work. I was torn between recording this extraordinary scene and, at the same time, anxious to return to the tactical operations on the dusty strips. Across the road was the first house to be liberated, a French café run by Monsieur and Madame Gondrée, who very kindly offered me a refreshing glass of wine, whilst recounting the stories of their ordeal under German occupation.

CONSOLIDATION – AND MOVING ON

O NCE A BRIDGEHEAD had been established in the summer of 1944 it was a question of consolidation, our positions stretching far along the coast, and constructing further airstrips. I was not far from B3 at Arromanches and Tilly. I learned that No 121 Wing was there and, not far away, the famous No 56 Squadron, now equipped with Typhoons.

The Germans had hitherto been virtually unmatched in their combination of air power and ground armour, and thus had conquered France relatively easily in 1940. Now, in 1944, having previously lost the Battle of Britain, the Germans were facing adversaries with superior air and land power. I wanted to be with the Typhoon squadrons when they began the counter-offensive. The next day I reported to the group captain of No 121 Wing, who welcomed me and introduced me to some of his pilots and the intelligence officers who would keep me informed of any action and assist me with transport, if necessary.

The German retreat from the beach-head began in August 1944. It was a No 268 Squadron pilot who sighted the initial mass retreat through Trun. He shot up some transport, which temporarily blocked the road and impeded the exodus for a short time. The Typhoons were called up to initiate the cab-rank attacks.

Falaise was the turning point after the hiatus at Caen, in which the resistance offered by the Germans seriously delayed the Allied breakthrough from the Cherbourg Peninsula. The enemy forces cracked in August and had started to run. Previously the German fighter force acted as the rearguard, but now our air power began to pulverise the fleeing columns of German troops as the RAF swept down the roads in front of them to halt their retreat. On every road they meted out to the German transport the punishment the Luftwaffe had inflicted on civilian traffic on the crowded roads of France in 1940.

Typhoons of No 83 Group were wreaking destruction never seen before. The German columns of trans-

port were trapped in bocage country where the roads were lined with high banks and tall hedges. The fire-power of the Typhoons with their rockets would stop a column of the routed army and another behind would effectively prevent its retreat. Hundreds of vehicles were burning, armoured cars and tanks were blown off the road. As each aircraft returned to rearm and refuel, its score was recorded on a blackboard mounted by the ground staff airmen, and figures began to mount as the days wore on. The Luftwaffe showed no appetite for combat and the RAF aircraft were queueing up to take their turn to complete the destruction. Amongst the debris of the German transport were large numbers of horse-drawn carts commandeered from the French, reminiscent of World War I. To me, the saddest sight of all were these unfortunate animals, caught up in the ruthless retreat and falling victims of air power.

Here we saw the result of a system developed where the air was definitely a part of the land battle. The reconnaissance wings with their army personnel directed fighter bombers to targets requiring immediate attention, even to a point where Typhoons would be sent ahead of the advance convoy to fire rockets into uncertain ground and photograph the traverse underground on infra-red film. The information, processed in a matter of minutes with the map reference, was radioed ahead instructing the heavy tanks where to cut corners. Our airstrips were now being abandoned for more open sites. The pace was rapid, for No 35 Wing found itself based at St Omer. The Germans were in full retreat, preceded by a pillar of smoke which after dark turned to flame when the RAF swept down the road in front of them.

LEAVING THE BEACH-HEAD

THE MOVE from the beach-head in August 1944 was one of the largest. I was invited to join the advance party travelling with Group Captain Anderson, commanding No 35 Photo Reconnaissance Wing, and the senior intelligence officer, Squadron Leader Laurence Irving. The journey through Caen was extremely slow as we picked our way through the rubble-piled streets impeded by the cratering and obstruction caused by the bombing. This was the heaviest and most concentrated air attack in support of ground forces ever attempted. Half the city had disappeared. Crossing the Seine over a very long Bailey bridge, Laurence Irving entered a small village boulangerie and reappeared triumphant waving two long french loaves, a pleasant change from the hard rations issued on these journeys. Butter was plentiful. The French would bring a large barrel into the Mess, knock off the iron bands holding the staves which would fall away leaving a four foot high mountain of butter standing in the Mess.

On arrival at Fresnoy Folny, the advance party and cooks had selected a spot for their field kitchen and were about to brew tea for the pilots who were due to arrive shortly. I went down to the village for some eggs and found it completely deserted. I knocked on the door of a house on a corner, which was opened by a child followed by its mother clasping two other young children showing obvious fear. I reassured her that I was British and wished only to purchase a few eggs. Her face brightened and she sent her oldest child to collect a dozen. I paid her what she asked in the currency of her country. The Germans printed their own French

currency, which had an extremely poor rate of exchange and was not so easily negotiable. Before I left, I gave the children some chocolate purchased from the American PX. (The PX was the equivalent of the British NAAFI.) As I returned to the airstrip, the first

aircraft were arriving, circling the airfield and awaiting permission to land.

A few days after our arrival, Laurence Irving mentioned that in a wood, clearly silhouetted on a hill, there was a V1 site, the first launching area we had come across. As it was less than two miles away, I walked up to the site. The wood was quite dense and, as I was about to enter a well-worn track just one vehicle wide, a truck drove out with some Canadians on board. They had just cleared the site of mines and told me that it was now wide open and safe. The track led to the centre of the wood, to the well-camouflaged launching ramp. The non-magnetic house, a thick concrete building, had been badly hit by our bombs.

The warheads were stored in a ski-shaped structure not far away. There were some cans of fuel shaped like over-large milk churns containing a 'lethal-looking yellow-green fluid. The launch trolley was in place, while outside the wood the grass was scarred by the trolley as it released the flying bomb. It was quite clear that it had been used frequently and not long before. There were skid marks on the grass at the edge of the wood where it had left the rails. I stayed to make some sketches.

On my return, I showed my sketches to some of the pilots and five of them, being off duty, drove up to the site. As I was showing the drawings to Laurence Irving, there was a tremendous explosion from the direction of the wood and a tall column of black smoke rose above the trees. The first pilot leaving the car had stepped on a mine. Fortunately, apart from losing his trousers and suffering split eardrums, he was not badly injured.

At St Omer airfield construction parties were clearing the ground and filling in the bomb craters left by our attack. Here we came across some curious triangular obstacles on solid wooden wheels. These were intended to prevent the airfield from being used by our aircraft, but the Germans had made such a hasty retreat, they had failed to employ them. Instead we used them to mark our craters on the perimeter tracks until they could be filled in.

Evidence of the hurried flight of the enemy was apparent from the half-eaten meals and personal possessions left behind. St Omer was the base for Adolf Galland's Me 109s and, later, the FW 190s. It was to the local hospital that Group Captain Douglas Bader was taken after he had been shot down in August 1941. Also, from this airfield, a signal was sent by the Germans to the British requesting a spare leg for Bader and, with it, an amnesty for the delivery aircraft.

For some time after the War, Adolf Galland insisted that the British not only dropped the artificial leg over St Omer, but also bombed the airfield. This was not so. There would be no point in dropping bombs at the same time as the leg for fear of damaging the limb. Nevertheless, belligerent bombs were dropped on Abbeville in response to the German offer of a free passage for the mission.

The Wing had moved in three stages from the region of the beach-head, B3 Beny-sur-Mer to Bernay, Bernay to St Omer, and then to Ghent. Whilst in Belgium, we were offered a large chateau near a river. It was a convent, the nuns were living in an annexe. This was the first time we had had a solid roof over our heads, as up to this point we had lived in tents. The rooms were large with very high ceilings, and our camp beds looked lost in such grand spaces. The officers decided

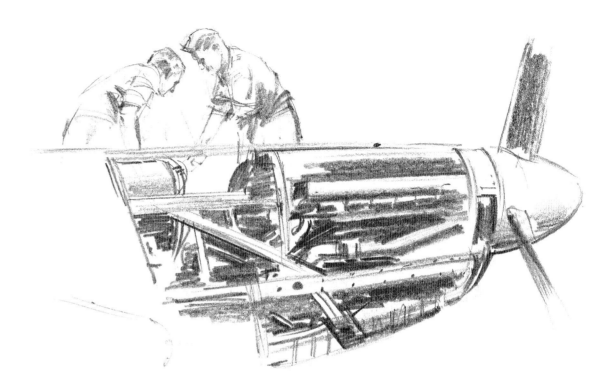

they should meet the locals to repay the hospitality we had received from the people of Ghent, and a dinner dance was arranged with some enthusiasm. Liquor was abundant and, by careful rationing, the squadron cooks were able to exercise their art on a grand scale. With the assistance of the Town Major, invitations were sent out to thirty girls of varying age and beauty, vouched for by the Mayors of Ghent.

As the women appeared, there was an air of apprehension. They formed a solid group at one end of the room, whilst the men were gathered at the opposite end around the bar. But not for long. The dance orchestra mustered from the town began to play some familiar popular tunes. Nothing happened for what seemed an interminable time, until someone made a move towards the group of women to start the dancing. This was the signal for everyone to fraternise on the dance floor. Later on it became all too apparent that the Town Major had provided an admixture of women, not all of them of impeccable virtue.

BELGIUM, 1944

THE LIBERATION of Brussels was followed by an invitation from the Belgian authorities to the liberators to avail themselves of the freedom of the city for three days.

On 2 October I drove from Ghent with Captain Palmer, staying overnight in one of the finest hotels in Brussels where we were dined and entertained without charge. The following day three American Mustangs arrived at our airfield and were parked at dispersal while their pilots borrowed a Jeep to drive to Brussels. A few days later two of the pilots returned, one of them a laconic Texan, who explained that his colleague, Joe, had met a girl in Brussels and was staying longer – would we burn his aircraft to defend his reluctant return? The group captain, who had admired the later mark of Mustang with an envious eye, instructed his ground crew to bring the aircraft over to the maintenance area where the substitution of British markings for American resolved the situation more economically.

Shortly afterwards, and with some regret, we left the ancient spires of Ghent and the comfort of a roof over our heads and, with the advance party, surveyed the dismal contrast of the rain-soaked airfield at Antwerp. There was extensive damage to the hangars and installations together with the usual squalid relics hurriedly left behind by the enemy. Nevertheless, it was cheering to see a row of Typhoons on the approach side of the airfield. We were to share the airfield with 126 Wing.

At this point, I received a signal recalling me to Supreme Headquarters, Bentley Priory. No reason was given. It was late October, and I flew back to England, my spirits at a low ebb. The Avro communications aircraft turned westward over the coast of France and I soon fell asleep, making up for the two nights I had lost getting to the departure stage. I awoke with a start. I had not strapped myself in and the aircraft was in a steep dive, an improbable manoeuvre for an Avro. Regaining my seat, I saw fabric tearing off the starboard wing, and heard the two Cheetah engines vibrating the aircraft as the pilot pushed open the throttles and steered into cloud cover. We were at no great altitude and, with no hope of reaching the shore, the pilot ditched the elderly Avro into a relatively calm sea. Air Sea Rescue was not long in reaching us and, fortuitously, my paintings were in three tubular waterproof containers which floated. Fortunately, we

were off the Sussex coast, not far from my home. I was able to stop a car and reach my house for a change of clothing before reporting to Bentley Priory.

I was summoned before Leigh-Mallory who told me that he had been appointed to command our air force in South-East Asia. He said the war in Europe would be over by Christmas and would I like to paint the jungle? He had acquired a new private aircraft, a York, and was flying out with a picked crew. His wife was to accompany him, also his batman, and a ton of personal luggage, and there would be room for me. Much as I wished to accept the offer, I hesitated. Urmston stood behind him nodding his head. However, I had to explain that I had left my painting equipment in Belgium unaware of the reason for my sudden return to England, to which he replied: 'Very well, come when you are ready. Urmston will make the necessary arrangements.'

I was asked to put on an impromptu exhibition of the work I had done in France at a farewell party Leigh-Mallory was giving to generals and other senior officers at SHAEF.

Leigh-Mallory never reached his new Command. His aircraft took off from Northolt on 14 November; a few hours later a faint signal reported that it was flying low, circling in a snowstorm. It crashed into a mountain south of Grenoble – all on board were killed.

In World War I Leigh-Mallory had commanded No 8 Squadron, and in World War II No 12 Group followed by No 11 Group of Fighter Command, the Fighter Command itself, and finally the Allied Expeditionary Air Force. His death was a great loss to the Royal Air Force.

I could do little but carry on finishing some of the work I had brought home from France. In the meantime Group Captain Urmston and Hilary St George Saunders who had introduced me to Leigh-Mallory were briefing the Air Ministry as to Leigh-Mallory's last directive to me.

It wasn't long before I was summoned to the Air Ministry in King Charles Street London. Group Captain Sir Willoughby de Broke was now Director of

Public Relations. After discussing the work I had been doing in France he said he would be making arrangements to get me out to the Far East as soon as possible.

The Headquarters of the South-East Asia Command was in Kandy, Ceylon. I thought it would be better if I could go straight to a squadron engaged in operations rather than incur further delays. This did not appear to create any undue administrative work and I left the Air Ministry looking forward to working in entirely different conditions abroad.

There was then the question of artists' materials to solve. All artists' materials were a problem during the war, and supplies were strictly limited. My work as an official artist made things a little easier and helped with the supply of canvas. However, I would not be able to replenish any materials so easily as I could when in France, owing to the great distance and limited transport.

Then I remembered that we were flying Hurricanes in Burma and if there was a shortage of canvas I might be able to prevail on Stores to let me have some off-cuts. The thought of a painting made on doped aircraft fabric certainly had a ring of authenticity about it.

INDIA, 1945

ON ARRIVAL IN INDIA I had a strong feeling that I had been there before, the buildings in Bombay, the natives and their dress, the sounds and smells and the unremitting sunshine appeared so familiar. Doubtless I had read books on the country and visited the British Empire Exhibition at Wembley in 1924 as a child, although none of these introductions had made any great impression.

I purchased a strong metal trunk with two padlocks in the bazaar. It took everything my kitbag held and appeared very much more secure. A young Indian boy

detached himself from a crowd of bearers and offered his services to carry my belongings to our transit camp. His name he told me was Younis. He was a small twelve-year-old. I tried to dismiss him, as he did not seem strong enough, but he protested it was nothing. All he needed was assistance to get the trunk on his head. No sooner had he spoken than two larger lads lifted the heavy trunk and placed it firmly on top of his head. Before I could protest, he had moved off, so that all I could do was to meekly follow my possessions. Although the journey through the dusty streets was the best part of a mile, he appeared just as unfatigued and happy as when he had started.

We had been given advice on payments for bearers and I assumed these were based on adult fees, so I increased the recommended amount and was pleased to see his face light up. He then offered his services as a permanent bearer and, after learning that I would not need one, as a final gesture, offered me the services of his sister, who he said was two years older than him and very beautiful.

After reporting to Public Relations, Calcutta, I was asked where I wanted to start work. I replied I did not mind as long as I could depict something of the RAF in action in the South-East Asia Command (SEAC). After a day or so, I was driven about a hundred miles north-west of Calcutta to Salbani, which was a bomber station. Previously I had always been sent to fighter squadrons, so I looked forward to meeting Nos 355 and 356 Squadrons flying Liberators, engaged at that time in bombing the docks at Rangoon.

After my escort had gone, the group captain welcomed me into his office and explained some of the work on which they were engaged. He said his station was wide open to me and I could begin when and where I liked; fortunately he knew something of my work. The climate here was less humid than that in Calcutta. I started work in the maintenance area to familiarise myself with the aircraft, as I had not seen a Liberator before. The distance from the bashar (a thatched bungalow) to the hangars was about two miles, a walk which I enjoyed; on more than one occasion I was hailed by friends I had met at a training station back in England. Later, I was to meet the son of Laurence Irving, John, who was a pilot, also another pilot, R. A. Jones, who lives very near to me in Sussex.

Salbani held a great deal of interest for me and the pace of my work quickened as I became familiar with the operations, favoured by the constant light day after day, the sun over the red laterite soil creating an entirely new palette for me.

The sun pens were something I had not seen before. They were specially constructed to house the nose, wings and engines of the Liberators, protecting the metal surfaces from the sun's rays. During the higher temperatures of 100°F–120°F, metal surfaces proved too dangerous for mechanics to work on safely. At either side was a dry mud wall which was roughly thatched. At first, I could not see what use they were, until one day the sky darkened and an incoming storm blew up with great force, bringing sand from the desert. A three-ton truck was caught just outside the wall and was blown into the side of one of the Liberators, causing considerable damage. I lost some of my work which was scattered over a wide area. Visibility was no more than a few yards. It was a most uncomfortable walk back to base, where considerable damage had taken place. Roofs were ripped off and trees uprooted. The following day everyone had recovered sufficiently to inspect the damage, the weather no longer hostile, but in contrast was in an even more tranquil mood than usual, as if repenting of the sudden tempest. I spent the day looking for my lost materials. Thankfully they were found undamaged, purely because I was using

100-octane fuel as a medium, which dried almost immediately in that climate.

There were so many subjects that came to mind which would have provided good material for a painting. For instance, at the beginning of the monsoon season a gang of Indians were employed 'puddle-kicking'. They would spread out across the runway, the foreman sporting a broken umbrella, a pair of old boots and a vest which showed more holes than material. His crowning glory was a hat which he wore with a great air of authority. Thus attired he gave the men their marching orders, walking along the whole length of the runway puddle-kicking with their bare feet, thus speeding up the normal evaporation rate by fifty percent.

If I had harboured any illusions about Calcutta, they would have been shattered by a brief talk given by an officer whose task was to brief newcomers to SEAC. Without wasting much time, he drew with considerable panache three or four bold strokes in chalk on a blackboard. He said: 'That is India, and here', he indicated in the top right hand corner, 'is the River Hooghly.' He paused briefly to explain that it was commonly known as the 'arsehole of India' and, with a final stroke that broke the chalk, 'and that is Calcutta which is half way up it.' He went on to explain some of the dangers and hazards the foolish and unwary were likely to meet.

It was a most unattractive place – a vast sprawl of closely knit buildings completely lacking any plan-

ning. The main street of Chowringee facing Victoria Park was a dismal imitation of Park Lane, London, a thin veneer backing on to slums. Most journeys west to east in India and vice versa passed through the local civil airport at Dum Dum. The back streets were fascinating. On one occasion, I watched an overloaded double-decker bus leaning precariously on the cambered road, festooned by Indians hanging on the outside all the way round the vehicle until not a single handhold was left. Suddenly a tyre bust under the gross overload. As I turned away, everyone including the hangers on, who had never intended to pay any fare, were demanding their money back from the unfortunate conductor, who clearly did not have enough fare money to fulfil their clamorous demands.

BURMA, 1945

THE BOMBER STATION at Salbani in India seemed very remote after the closer tactics in Normandy, so after I had made a number of paintings of the aircraft in action and some studies in the maintenance area I asked the station commander if he could arrange transport to an airfield in Rangoon where some of our fighters were deployed. He agreed and introduced me to a tall Air Force officer wearing a Victoria Cross ribbon. He was James Nicholson, who asked me to look after his dog while he flew on a watching brief with the squadron bombing the harbour at Rangoon.

I flew down to Rangoon by Dakota, a memorable flight in monsoon weather. The aircraft was unable to fly above the banks of storm clouds, the peaks of the teak-covered hills were swathed in cloud, so that only now and again was it possible to see the hills below or the sky above. As the Dakota was carrying two enormous field guns, the seats had been removed and I sat on the metal floor with the guns weighing several tons tugging and jerking at the webbing that held them in place as the aircraft staggered through the turbulence. We landed just outside Rangoon at Mingladon, flooded after the monsoon rain.

I joined No 607 Squadron, equipped with Spitfires. Even when landing, the additional hazard of a flooded airfield caused fighter aircraft to tip over on to their nose, bend propellors, and sometimes damage the reduction gear. Whatever your job, working in such conditions was not easy. It was hot and humid; leather turned green overnight, blankets and sheets were constantly damp, amenities were few, food monotonous

and housing uncomfortable. However, the promise of victory with the advent of Spitfire squadrons steadily improved morale.

I flew to Mandalay to paint the destruction of Fort Dufferin, the ancient home of Burmese kings. Thunderbolts, Hurricanes and Mitchells, carrying 500lb bombs, three on each aircraft, breached the 45ft walls of the fort. It was while painting these aircraft taking off heavily laden with 1,500lb of bombs that one detached itself from its holding just as the aircraft lifted off the rough track, and the bomb hit the ground no more than thirty feet in front of me. It skipped over my head and finally came to rest in some soft earth a few yards away. As I was gathering up my things to beat a hasty retreat, a truck drew up alongside. I was told in no uncertain terms to jump aboard and we sped away

When a Thunderbolt's bomb-carrier sheared on taking-off owing to the rough surface . . .

. . . it came to rest within 50 yards of the artist. 'Even painting', recalled Frank Wootton, 'had its moments!'

at breakneck speed. By some good fortune, I do not think it exploded.

About thirty-five years later, by a happy coincidence, I was at the Guild of Aviation Artists' Exhibition in London when a man introduced himself. He explained his name was Wallace and that he was flying the Thunderbolt which dropped the bomb that so narrowly missed me in Burma that day.

After the fall of Mandalay, IV Corps advanced eighty-five miles to Meiktila. The capture of Meiktila was a great victory for General Slim and the nodal point of the battle for Burma. Four hundred men of the Royal Air Force Regiment shared the defence of the airfield. We lost a great many Dakotas which were flying in tons of food and ammunition. I flew to Meiktila in an Auster, dropping mail at small airstrips en route. At Mingladon I had been off-loaded from a Dakota which had started moving along the runway to take off when it was stopped. The aircraft was full and a brigadier on an important mission had requested a seat. As I was the only single passenger on board, I got out and was offered a seat in an Auster mail plane. Flying quite low from one grass strip to another was much more fun, even though at the end of most of them were usually a few hideous-looking vultures. Arriving at Meiktila, I was directed to a small tin-roofed hut and explained I had been taken off the Dakota flight and just arrived by mail plane. The sergeant-in-charge looked at me with an amused expression on his face: 'You're effing lucky, mate. That Dakota is five hours overdue.' In fact, it never did arrive.

I set to work at Meiktila with renewed vigour. The contrast of clear blue skies and sun from the monsoon mud of Mingladon was like a tonic. There was also an exhilarating breeze that disturbed the bells on nearby temples, a languid tintinnabulation contrasting with the roar of the aircraft from the airfield. I painted the busy staging post and the ubiquitous Dakotas, unloading stores and supplies, from the balcony of the wooden control tower perched high up on teak logs. Nearby was a large lake dotted with islands, on which were some small pagodas looking most attractive in the tropical sun. A few of us were tempted to swim. Unfortunately we did not get very far, as just below the surface we discovered the lake was filled with Japanese corpses. While dressing, I noticed the RAF water bowser at the edge of the lake pumping up water into its tank. I asked the driver what it was to be used for. He replied I would be drinking it that night. Most of us in the mess that evening chose gin and tonic.

Meiktila, Burma

I RECOLLECT A MARVELLOUS DAY, during a lull between operations, driving with four of the pilots to see a bridge they had bombed. We had a three-ton truck and 4½ gallon 'jerricans' for seats. The journey of about eighty-five miles was made over rough tracks through the jungle. We found the bridge well and truly out of commission and looked like remaining so for the duration of the war. On the return journey darkness fell swiftly as it does in the tropics and, due to the terrain, we lost the track. Eventually, we came across a stockade heavily barricaded with high, closely-built tree trunks. Driving around it, we found a solid gateway noisily guarded by dogs. We directed our headlights at the doorway and some hastily shouted

orders from inside gathered the dogs under control. Eventually, the great gate opened a few inches. One of our party explained that we were lost and asked for directions. We were welcomed in and taken to an English-speaking Burmese gentleman who explained that he was the Commissioner of Rangoon in hiding from the Japanese. He was an excellent host and we were invited to join him for a meal. We ate on the balcony of his very attractive house, drinking fresh lime juice sweetened with honey. The meal was prepared and consisted of about sixteen different dishes or courses. The conversation was both amusing and interesting. Behind each guest stood two beautifully dressed minute Burmese women, one bringing small dishes of food and the other removing each dish when finished. Our host enquired about our occupations in the RAF, and on learning that I was an artist requested a quick pencil sketch of his very beautiful daughter and her baby to send to her husband who was fighting in the Chin Hills and so far had not seen his infant daughter. They were both delighted with the drawing and we were invited to return.

We eventually took our leave. The commissioner

said he would provide us with a guide who would travel with us until we were once again on familiar ground. On returning to our truck, we found it filled with baskets containing live ducks, a handsome present indeed, for our food in the Far East was pretty dismal, consisting of the barest essentials augmented by assorted pills – vitamin, salt and Mepacrine.

On 6 August 1945, while I was still at Meiktila, the first atomic bomb was dropped on Hiroshima, and on 9 August a second bomb fell on Nagasaki. On 14 August Japan accepted the Allied demand for unconditional surrender. This remarkable and awe-inspiring achievement was met at first with composure, almost disbelief. On the station notice board a buff sheet of paper announced the fact officially. There was to be a celebration during which a whole ox was to be roasted and free rum issued. The ox was skewered with a long iron rod supported on two aircraft jacks. A Japanese gun wheel on each end of the iron rod turned the carcase over at intervals over a wood fire kept stoked with timber. In the evening the rum was ladled into pint mugs, Group Captain Key gave a short Victory speech and cut the first slice of meat. From then on it was self service. In the mad rush, the carcase was seen to be lifted off the jacks with airmen hacking off large chunks of beef. I saw what was left of it next morning; the ribcage and a few odd bones were several hundred yards away. What the airmen had not eaten, the vultures had finished off.

Shortly after VJ Day, I received a signal from HQ SEAC to report to SEAC Headquarters at Kandy, Ceylon. I regretted having to leave and mentioned this fact to the commanding officer, who gently reminded me that these signals sometimes took weeks to arrive in the jungle. I thanked him and stayed a little longer completing some unfinished work.

During this time, the Wing organised a competition for the best design for a Victory poster. This was announced in Daily Routine Orders. While reading it, I noticed at the bottom of the announcement the words 'Wootton Barred', but I was invited to help judge the competition.

KANDY, CEYLON, 1945

EVENTUALLY I LEFT for Calcutta, where I stayed overnight before flying down to Kandy. While waiting in the early hours of the morning for a Service bus to take me to Dum Dum Airport, I happened to see a notice on the hotel notice board which read 'The Grand Hotel is out of bounds to all Service personnel owing to an outbreak of cholera'. I had wondered why it was so unusually empty.

Kandy was a refreshing change as the train wound its way up into the interior along a very scenic route through tree-clad hills. There was a relaxed atmosphere among the personnel now that the war was over. One of the most urgent requirements was to fly former prisoners of war home. A further consideration was to

keep the airmen occupied until their return home could be organised. I was asked to put on an impromptu exhibition of my work. To this end, I was allotted a large thatched hut normally used for social occasions and, with the aid of a few NCOs who willingly mustered some large screens, the canvasses were unrolled and pinned flat and the unsightly tacked edges framed with masking tape.

Great interest was shown. The Commander-in-Chief, Sir Keith Park, arrived and I was introduced to him. We went round the exhibition together while I explained where some of the works had been painted. There were a few portraits and I was delighted when Sir Keith named some of them he had known from the Battle of Britain.

Afterwards, the C-in-C congratulated me on my work. Then Sir Keith asked me what I intended to do now that the war was over. I said I would like to en-

large some of the paintings, since due to the working conditions and shortage of materials I had of necessity worked on a much smaller scale than I would have liked. He replied 'I am afraid we have no facilities here to offer you. I think it best you should return home', and, turning to Group Captain Dodds, asked him to see that I was flown home as soon as possible.

Within a very short time I was aboard a Dakota bound for Karachi, where there was a Sunderland flying-boat due to leave for the United Kingdom. As I went through Immigration a doctor, looking at my 1250 [RAF Form 1250 – identity card, carried at all times] and recognising my name, showed me two consecutive copies of *The Calcutta Statesmen*. The entire back pages were filled with reproductions of my paintings.

On the morning of 25 July 1915, Captain Hawker, flying a British Scout C of No 6 Squadron RFC, mounted an obliquely-aligned Lewis gun on his aircraft. He drove down three enemy two-seaters in the course of a single patrol. For this action he was awarded the Victoria Cross, the first such award for an action in aerial combat.

Presented to No 6 Squadron RAF by the artist

CAPTAIN LANOE G. HAWKER

SE5a aeroplanes of No 56 Squadron in France preparing to take off. The aircraft marked with a large 'G' is McCudden's machine B4863 which he flew in October 1917.

During his service with No 56 Squadron, McCudden led his flight on more than seventy patrols, during which he shot down twenty-five enemy aircraft. He also claimed twenty-seven enemy aircraft during freelance special missions. Altogether, he was accredited with fifty-seven victories.

By courtesy of the Royal Air Force Club

Germany's ace of aces, Manfred von Richthofen, in his scarlet
Fokker Dr1 triplane is heavily engaged with British SE5as.

Richthofen must have fought his way out of many such battles,
for his victory score was eighty before his last flight, which took
place on 9 April 1918 between Sailly le Sec and Le Hamel. Captain
Roy Brown of Canada was credited by many with shooting down
Richthofen on that day.

By kind permission of Tim Rutter, Esq.

ENCOUNTER WITH THE RED BARON, 1918.
36in x 25in

Most likely a BE12a around 1918, a very stable machine in the
right hands. No disrespect to the pilot. His motor may have cut
out on take-off.

By kind permission of Victor Gauntlett, Esq.

The Vickers-Vimy, powered by two 360hp Rolls Royce Eagle engines, was piloted by Captain John Alcock and Lieutenant Arthur Whitten Brown of the Royal Air Force. Starting their flight on 14 June 1919, they landed in Ireland at 8.40am on 15 June, having taken sixteen hours and twelve minutes, giving an average ground speed of 188 miles per hour.

By courtesy of the Fleet Air Arm Museum, Yeovilton

THE FIRST NON-STOP TRANSATLANTIC FLIGHT
36in x 25in

THE CHINA CLIPPER

22in x 16in

On 22 November 1935, the China Clipper with Eddie Musick at the controls, took off from San Francisco Bay heading for Hawaii. The aircraft carried mail. The initial run was 2,400 miles, the longest over-water flight at that time. The unfinished Golden Gate Bridge can be seen in the background.

By kind permission of Jiri Srail, Esq.

In 1986 I met Sir Humphrey Edwardes-Jones, the first RAF officer to fly the Spitfire on 26 May 1936, the day it was delivered.

Air Marshal Sir Wilfred Freeman, the Air Member for Research and Development, The Air Council, had more-or-less agreed to place an order for the Spitfire provided the council could be satisfied on two points: first, that the aircraft could achieve its designed speed of 350mph, and second, that it could safely be flown by the ordinary Service-trained pilot.

On the day that test pilot Mutt Summers flew the aircraft to Martlesham, Edwardes-Jones, then a flight lieutenant, was told by his commanding officer that he was to fly the Spitfire that afternoon. Afterwards, he was to telephone Air Marshal Sir Wilfred Freeman at the Air Ministry. When the aircraft had been refuelled, E.J, as he was known, was given a short cockpit briefing. He then flew the aircraft as instructed. After the flight, he telephoned Sir Wilfred, who seemed interested in only one question: was the aeroplane, in E.J.'s opinion, capable of being flown safely by the ordinary Service-trained fighter pilots? E.J. replied yes, provided that they had been instructed on the use of retractable undercarriages, flaps and other systems on the new types of aircraft coming into RAF service, they would have no difficulty with the Spitfire, which was a delight to fly. One week later, on 3 June 1936, the first production order was signed for 310 Spitfires.

Edwardes-Jones was not told at the time of the significance of his report. Fortunately for everyone concerned his answer proved right. In the circumstances, time was short. He could not possibly have known the importance of his evaluation, but later, in the course of events, he must have realised the part he played in deciding the future security of the country.

By kind permission of Victor Gauntlett, Esq.

BERT HINKLER CROSSING THE SOUTH ATLANTIC

On 25 November 1931, 'Bert' Hinkler, an Australian, left Natal, Brazil, to make the first west-to-east South Atlantic crossing by air. He was flying a de Havilland Puss Moth with a 120hp Gipsy III engine.

In twenty-two hours, he had crossed 1,890 miles of open sea to Bathurst, Gambia.

By courtsey of the de Havilland Aircraft Company

UNARMED AGAINST THE ENEMY

The first photo reconnaissance Spitfire I saw was operating in France in 1944. I was with No 35 PR Wing, which at the time was equipped with Spitfires, Typhoons and Mustangs, each having a special role in photo reconnaissance. The Spitfires were used for high-altitude work, and the Mustangs for low-level obliques. They were required to photograph the entire front line daily. While in France, I remember painting the sky-blue Spitfire operating at high altitude and recording the Mustang working at low level.

After the war, I met Air Chief Marshal Sir Neil Wheeler, who was my host in Singapore. We talked at some length about his early days with Wing Commander Geoffrey Tuttle who commanded the Heston Flight. The high-level flights were usually carried out at twenty to thirty thousand feet, unarmed, unheated, with no radio, penetrating enemy territory hopefully undetected. One of the greatest problems was to avoid leaving telltale condensation trails. Before cockpit heating was installed, extreme cold was another problem. It was a vitally important activity, carried out from 1939 until the cessation of hostilities.

By kind permission of Air Chief Marshal Sir Neil Wheeler, GCB, CBE, DSO, DFC, AFC.

The North West Frontier was the land border of the Empire across which invasion was most feared – Afghanistan to the west and Soviet Russia to the north. A typical routine operation undertaken by No 11 Squadron was to fly up to Gilgit, the object being to give support to the Political Agent stationed there, also to deliver and collect important mail.

No 11 Squadron was based at Risalpur, India. Its aircraft were constantly in action against marauding tribesmen. British aircraft were first engaged on the Frontier Province in 1915 and figure prominently in later campaigns, effectively maintaining internal security at the same time, with considerable economies in frontier warfare.

I flew to Gilgit in 1968 and painted the background. Nanga Parbat can be seen in the distance. The Hawker Hart was much nearer home, kept in flying condition at Dunsfold, Surrey, and frequently flown by the Harrier test pilot, Mr Duncan Simpson.

Presented to the Royal Air Force Museum by the artist

ADLERTAG

Hurricanes taking off from an airfield near London. The airfield
has been badly bombed. There was no time to infill the bomb
craters, which were marked with yellow flags. An Me109 has
been brought down, crashing into the boundary hedge; the pilot,
unhurt, is being taken away by the intelligence officers while the
battle is still being fought overhead.

Presented to Dowding House, RAFA, by the artist

42

On this day, the Germans flew over 1,000 sorties and lost fifty-six aircraft. British losses were twenty-six. The Luftwaffe failed completely to deliver the knockout blow.

By 18 September the Germans had assembled more than one thousand barges at the Channel Ports in preparation for 'Operation Sealion', the threatened invasion of England.

On 17 September, the German War Headquarters recorded 'The enemy air force is still by no means defeated; on the contrary, it shows increasing activity. The Fuhrer, therefore, decides to postpone "Sealion" indefinitely.'

By kind permission of Victor Gauntlett, Esq.

BATTLE OVER LONDON,
15 SEPTEMBER 1940
36in x 25in

DOWN ON THE FARM
36in x 25in

Just after lunch on 21 August 1940, Wing Commander Robert Doe was scrambled against a raid in the Winchester area. Aided by good ground control, he was vectored within sight of a German Ju88 bomber seeking cloud cover at low level.

'He must have seen me at about the same time; due to my superior manœuvrability I was able to close up behind him. I could see tracer coming in my direction. It's funny how it seems to start off slowly straight towards you, then speeds up and veers away at the last moment. Having closed right up on him to about two hundred yards, I fired a long burst. He ceased firing and the bomber sank slowly towards the ground, crashing in a farm field at King's Somborne in Hampshire.'

By kind permission of Jan Endresen, Esq.

The pilot is seen signing Form 700 before taking-off. One of the ground crew is running-up the engine. Hurricane pilots were frequently called upon to undertake missions which were outside the normal span of daylight operations.

There were eight squadrons of Hurricanes and Defiants although, later with sophisticated airborne radar equipment, the techniques of interception at night were developed using twin-engined aircraft and an air interceptor observer, navigator. It was a highly specialised technique. One of the most famous exponents was Squadron Leader John Cunningham who flew a Beaufighter together with Sergeant C.F. Rawnsley in 1941, soon becoming the outstanding night-fighter crew of the war.

By courtesy of RAF Strike Command

NIGHT WORK, 1940

LOOKING FOR TROUBLE
36in x 25in

An early formation assiduously practised pre-war by RAF fighter pilots until 1939-40, but later changed to a finger-four formation which had greater advantages. The aircraft were also painted half black and half white underneath, but this was altered at a later date to duck-egg green.

By kind permission of Victor Gauntlett, Esq.

JOHN DUNDAS
30in x 20in

When it was based at Biggin Hill, I visited RAF No 609 Squadron, City of Yorkshire, famous for being the first to score one hundred enemy aircraft. I was welcomed by Squadron Leader Michael Robinson who introduced me to several of the pilots. One sensed immediately that it was a very happy unit and one of the most enthusiastic with whom I had the pleasure of working. The first painting I made here was the reconstruction of a combat between John Dundas and Major Wick of the Luftwaffe, who had fifty-seven victories to his credit – John had twelve.

On 28 November 1940, John had been stood down by the medical officer. However, on this day, the squadron was scrambled to engage a large formation of enemy aircraft over the Isle of Wight. On the pretext of testing his Spitfire, John took off, catching up with the squadron and joining in the battle. No-one saw him shoot down Major Wick, but he was heard to say over the radio 'I've got a 109' and then went silent. Someone reported a German aircraft falling in to the sea. The squadron members were devastated to learn that he failed to return, having been shot down by Major Wick's No 2. That night the German radio asked for any news of Major Wick, confirming that he too had been shot down.

By kind permission of No 609 Squadron

46

In 1940, when home on leave from the RAF, I painted the background of this picture, as I had just moved into a cottage next to the barn seen on the right.

Horses were used at the time and, during the Battle of Britain, became targets for returning German fighters, whose pilots wished to expend all their ammunition, as it was counted on their return to base. Naturally, the horses became restive on hearing approaching aircraft, although both the animals and ploughmen were soon able to distinguish between the sound of friend and foe.

By kind permission of Wing Commander Patrick Coulcher

STEADY, THERE –
THEM'S SPITFIRES!
30in x 26in

THE BATTLE OF THE DINGHY

30in x 20in

On 8 May 1941 No 609 Squadron was scrambled again and vectored to a dinghy which contained a German airman. An Air Sea Rescue launch had been despatched to bring the pilot in. A German rescue launch was also on the scene, and a battle for the unfortunate airman ensued. The British launch was set on fire, while overhead a large number of Me109s circled the launches and dinghy.

No 609 Squadron arrived on the scene to join in the battle. Two Me109s were shot down with no loss to the squadron. The German rescue boat was also seen off, leaving the British Air Sea Rescue boat to bring in the captured German pilot.

By kind permission of No 609 Squadron

Fairey Swordfish of the Fleet Air Arm from the aircraft carrier *Illustrious* attacked the Italian fleet in Taranto Harbour. In one night, the Fleet Air Arm inflicted a greater amount of damage on the enemy than did Nelson at the Battle of Trafalgar, and nearly twice as much as the entire British Fleet at the Battle of Jutland in World War I. Eleven torpedoes left the Italian fleet a spent force.

By courtesy of the Fleet Air Arm Museum, Yeovilton

TARANTO,
11 NOVEMBER 1940

WING COMMANDER BOB STANFORD TUCK, DSO, DFC. 'ONE OFF SMARTLY'

36in x 25in

Bob was a great friend of mine. I had known him for many years. We often travelled together to the USA where we took part in a symposium at the National Air and Space Museum in Washington – one of the first, for they became very popular.

We visited Germany where he met an old friend and adversary, Adolf Galland. We attended a Jägdflieger-Treffen in Munich in October 1979, a unique occasion as there must have been more than 900 fighter pilots from all over the world gathered there.

In Bermuda we collected a substantial sum of money for the RAF Museum. A number of prints were jointly published by us, which also brought benefits to the RAF Museum and other charities.

By kind permission of A. Baldocchi, Esq.

In April 1941, Raschid Ali, an Iraqi rebel backed by four generals, seized power in Baghdad. The deposed Regent, Abdullah Illa, fled for protection to the Royal Air Force at Habbaniya. Raschid Ali and his generals were known to be backed by the Germans, their objectives being to deny access to the oilfields of Iraq and Persia and to advance on Egypt from an entirely new direction. Two-hundred-and-thirty women and children also fled Baghdad, seeking RAF protection at Habbaniya, where there were no operational units, just No 4 Flying Training School under the Air Officer Commanding, Iraq, Air Vice-Marshal H.G. Smart. The training aircraft were about sixty Audaxes, officially capable of carrying eight 20lb bombs but now armed to take two 250lb bombs with safety, and a few Oxfords which were not capable of operating under wartime conditions.

Raschid Ali's forces comprised around 6,000 to 7,000 men, many light tanks, armoured cars and field guns. He also had fifty first-line aircraft and German support of Me110s and Italian Cr42s. Together with a few advanced pupils, the Royal Air Force instructors flew some 1,400 sorties against the enemy. The battle began on 1 May and the siege was broken by the end of the month. Raschid Ali's brief spell of power was ended. On 30 May, the Regent was escorted in triumph to his capital. No 4 Flying Training School had saved Iraq, the Persian oilfields, and the supply road from Ahwaz to Russia was now safeguarded. Three weeks later Germany went to war with Russia.

By kind permission of No 4 Flying Training School Valley

GROUP CAPTAIN DOUGLAS BADER, CBE, DSO, DFC.
36in x 25in

Douglas naturally preferred this painting to *Bader Bale Out*, commenting, 'a bloody good deflection shot'.

BADER BALE OUT
36in x 25in

Douglas was a legendary figure, colourful and controversial. He was a distinguished fighter leader of World War II and one of England's greatest heroes.

I painted the picture entitled *Bader Bale Out* at the suggestion of a mutual friend, Wing Commander Bob Stanford Tuck. It was 9 August 1941. A number of things had gone wrong; the incident has been covered by many writers, but controversy still remains as to how it happened.

Bader always thought he was hit by an Me109 in a collision, the only feasible explanation as the whole rear portion of his Spitfire has been torn away. Galland told me 'There was no collision. He was shot down.' One is reminded of the controversy which still surrounds the mystery as to how Baron von Richthofen was shot down in world War I.

On reflection, two good things mitigated the unhappy day. Douglas survived and returned after the war, and the painting was sold for £6,000 by the RAF Benevolent Fund to The National Air and Space Museum in Washington, DC, the proceeds being used to support the funding of the Duke of Kent School near Ewhurst, Surrey, where priority is given to children whose fathers have died or been killed while serving in the Royal Air Force.

Presented to the Royal Air Force Benevolent Fund by the artist

174 Squadron flying from Manston in 1942.

Painted to launch a limited edition of prints to assist The Blenheim Restoration Fund. John Romain and Graham Warner, together with a team of voluntary helpers, are undertaking the restoration of the one and only Blenheim at the British Aerial Museum at Duxford.

By kind permission of Lord Rothermere

FLYING OFFICER FANE DISCOVERS *TIRPITZ*

30in x 20in

On 23 January 1942, Flying Officer A.F.P. Fane of No 1 Photographic Reconnaissance Unit was searching for the *Tirpitz*.

He had flown along the west coast of Norway as far as Trondheim and his fuel was nearing the limit of the point of no return. He carried on to Afjord, which at first appeared empty. But his curiosity was aroused by something indistinguishable close to the shore. He flew along the opposite side of the fjord taking oblique photographs. He was able to see it was indeed the *Tirpitz*, clearly camouflaged from ship to shore by netting covered in snow. He took several photographs from the opposite side of the fjord without inviting any opposition. He then flew lower to between two and three hundred feet, passing over the ship taking vertical photographs. Surprisingly, he was able to get away without being fired upon.

By kind permission of John Aldington, Esq.

Originally conceived as an unarmed bomber with fighter speed. On 15 May 1941 the Mosquito prototype, W4050, flew for the first time. Until early 1944 it proved to be faster than any other aircraft in the world. The RAF flew its first Mosquito sortie on 20 September 1941. Mosquitos had several roles in the war; photo reconnaissance, night fighting, bombing, and special operations involving pinpoint attacks using a precise bomb sight called 'Oboe' on individual buildings, such as Amiens Gaol, Gestapo Headquarters in Copenhagen and many others.

Being constructed mainly in wood, the Mosquito gave only a very faint signal on the German radar sets. At the same time, the German fighters were practically powerless against the Mosquito, due to its very high speed. Indirectly it was the outstanding performance of this aircraft which caused Hitler to delay the oper-ational status of the Me262, the jet twin-engined German fighter. In December 1943 Hitler, having watched an early demonstration of the Me262, asked Göring; 'Can this aircraft carry bombs?' Göring replied; 'Yes, my Führer.' Hitler said; 'At last, this is the "Blitz Bomber".' The conversion from fighter to bomber caused unforseen problems with centre of gravity, fuel consumption, bomb sights and other factors. Already, eighteen months had been lost in the production of the Me262, and it was October 1944 before the aircraft was allocated to German fighter units for service.

I flew with Geoffrey de Havilland while test flying the Mosquito when on attachment from the RAF.

In the artist's collection

THE MOSQUITO

57

PEENEMUNDE
72in x 60in

On the night of 17/18 August 1943 Bomber Command launched an attack on the highly secret German research station of Peenemunde. It was one of the most important and effective of World War II. The Germans were developing an advanced form of rocket projectile and a pilotless aeroplane, which they planned to launch in vast numbers to destroy London and other cities within range. The military experimental station at Peenemunde began development in 1937 on what was formerly a nature reserve on the Baltic coast.

The selection of the target was the direct responsibility of Commander-in-Chief Air Chief Marshal Sir Arthur Harris, with directive from the Chief of Air Staff: 'If you don't knock out this important target tonight, it will be laid on again tomorrow and every night until the job is done.' The significance of these words was not lost on the Pathfinder crews of No 83 Squadron assembled for briefing on the afternoon of 17 August, 1943.

The plan of the night was well conceived. The weather was fine, a bright moonlit night that could be friendly initially for bombers, but which on balance would also serve the cause of the German night fighters. Eight Mosquitos of No 139 Squadron would make a diversionary strike on Berlin an hour before the

attack began on Peenemunde with the object of drawing the German fighters away from the area. The main force of bombers, 597 aircraft from thirty-six Squadrons were detailed to attack this high priority target. The force attacked from 12,000ft in three waves, each having a separate aiming point. The master bomber, Air Commodore John Searby, remained over the target at 6,000ft throughout, issuing instructions to aircraft as they arrived, dropping coloured marker flares to illuminate vital target areas – a complicated operation and one which demanded the utmost accuracy and timing from the Pathfinder crews. Much of the station was devastated and a number of highly important buildings destroyed. Forty-one bombers were lost in conditions especially favourable to the night fighters.

John Searby was awarded the Distinguished Service Order immediately after the raid in recognition of 'gallantry displayed in flying operations against the enemy'. (Extract from the master bomber's flying log book).

To achieve an accurate construction of the painting, I initially consulted Air Commodore H. Probert, the Air Historian of the Royal Air Force, while at the painting stage the master bomber himself visited me in my studio, staying with me to see the work finished. On his return home, he wrote to me: 'The painting is thrilling: my Lancaster dominates the scene, faithfully reproduced and ALIVE! (I can hear the roar of the Merlins). Because the main opposition came from the enemy fighters, who knocked down 40 of our number, at least one, either SE or twin-engined (ME110), should be seen. The flak ships – two – were visible, faintly, and the oncoming bombers in the background, tho' I appreciate the difficulty in showing them. Over the target I witnessed seven destroyed . . . during the second or third phase.

'This is going to be a great picture and a lasting tribute to those who didn't come home again. I only wish Sir Arthur were alive to see it. It would have sweetened his last days. The painting helps to put right the neglect of the sacrifice of 50,000 Officers and NCOs of Bomber Command, and is to be hailed as such.' (Air Commodore John Searby DSO, DFC.)

By kind permission of the Royal Air Force Club

THE MÖHNE DAM, 1943 (*Opposite*)
36in x 25in

No 617 Squadron attacking the Möhne Dam on the night of 16/17 May 1943. The dam had a surface area of ten square kilometres and a maximum depth of one hundred and five feet. It contained over 130 million tons of water supplying pumping stations and electrical plants in the Ruhr. The wall of the dam was twenty-five feet thick at the top and one hundred and twelve feet at the base.

Under the command of Wing Commander Guy Gibson, the attack carried out by nineteen aircraft dropped a special type of bomb designed by the scientist Dr Barnes Wallis. The raid was successful although the crews encountered heavy anti-aircraft fire both from the shore and the towers of the dam.

On his return, Gibson was awarded the Victoria Cross. There were a number of Australians among the attacking crews. This painting now hangs in the National War Museum, Canberra,

Australia. Under the painting is a large bronze plate giving details of the Möhne Dam. when it was built, the maker's name and other information – a souvenir collected by the Australians after the fall of Germany.

To make this painting, the RAF flew me over the Möhne Dam, by coincidence on the 34th anniversary of the raid.

By courtesy of the Australian War Memorial Art Collection, Canberra

LANCASTER
36in x 25in

Lancaster aircraft based in Lincolnshire, crossing the North Sea in the late evening sun. The early start would indicate a long haul to the target area. As they left the rendezvous point on the coast of Norfolk, the crews would have been busy checking the intercom system, the flight engineer the engine revs and oil pressures, while the gunners, swinging their turrets from side to side, kept a close watch on the skies ahead.

It would be dark over Holland. Away to the right, the twinkle of anti-aircraft shells from guns in the Rotterdam area. From small towns in Holland friendly Dutchmen would risk all by blinking lights to the aircraft passing overhead. The enemy would be watching the numerous small blips on their radar screens, their night-fighter squadron crews buckling on their parachutes for the impending battle.

In the artist's collection

60

In 1943, there were many occasions when solitary Flying Fortresses dropped out of their formations owing to damaged engines, flight controls, etc.

In August 1943, at about 5.00pm, 'Johnnie' Johnson was escorting a crippled Fortress returning from a raid on Germany. He was flying a Spitfire Mark 9 at a height of about a thousand feet above the Fortress when he saw an Me109 come out of a cloud, preparing to attack the bomber. Levelling out from his long dive at high speed, they both turned over the 'straggler' until another

Spitfire appeared, when the German aircraft turned quickly away and disappeared back into a cloud. Not a shot was fired.

Some time after the war, the two pilots met and were reminiscing about that time. On comparing flying log books, 'Johnnie' discovered that the yellow-nosed Me109F was flown by none other than Adolf Galland.

By kind permission of John Ray, Esq.

THE STRAGGLER
36in x 25in

FRIDAY 13th
36in x 25in

Since this painting was published as a print, I received several letters from pilots and crews who had flown in the aircraft. It made 128 sorties and returned at the end of the war to go on display outside John Lewis' store in Regent Street, London.

It was delivered to No 158 Squadron on a Friday 13th some time between December 1943 and May 1945. This was regarded by some as a foreboding omen for a short life, albeit that the life expectancy of any bomber was not long. The nose of the aircraft was painted with bad luck symbols, a skull and crossbones, an inverted horseshoe and a little 'Friday 13th'. Superstition was proved wrong. The aircraft never faltered and survived the war with 128 operational sorties, the largest number of bomber raids recorded for a single aircraft. Eventually it was broken-up, but the nose panel was saved for the RAF Museum.

By kind permission of Victor Gauntlett, Esq.

A very famous aircraft of World War II. The prototype HP57 first flew on 25 October 1939. The first squadrons entered service in November 1943. They were used for daylight bombing as well as by night. After VE Day, Halifaxes were sent to the Far East.

My painting shows a damaged Halifax limping home on three engines.

By kind permission of Alan Etherington, Esq.

HALIFAX BIII
36in x 25in

During the war, the essence of surprise when approaching enemy shores was to fly low under their radar beams. Pulling up to gain height for bombing, the Lancasters are caught in the lowered searchlights.

By kind permission of Alan Etherington, Esq.

Painted for the Irving Airchute Company, whose parachutes have saved the lives of thousands of airmen. I think the best description of this painting comes from an anglophile, Gordon Goudy, who now lives in America. He wrote to me saying: 'It was a shock when I looked at your print of "Lancaster Bale Out". I was a pilot officer tail gunner in 619 Squadron Five Group Bomber Command. We were shot down over Heilbronn, Germany, on 4th December, 1944 and I was the only survivor. The picture is just the way I remember my last view of our aircraft. The flames are exactly right, the sky, the lights perfect!'

By courtesy of the RAF Bomber Museum

LANCASTER BALE OUT
30in x 22in

MUSTANG OF NO 2 SQUADRON, 35 WING, PHOTOGRAPHING A V1 SITE IN NORMANDY

Early reconnaissance photographs of Rocket installations in October and November 1943 revealed the extent of Germany's plan to launch pilotless aircraft or V1 bombs against London.

The whole of the French coast from Cherbourg to Calais was photographed. One hundred and seventy-six sites, all facing across the Channel were identified. Each site was slightly different, but contained a ramp aligned in the direction of London. The ski-shaped concrete buildings housed the warheads; the open end was curved to prevent the repercussion damaging the whole store from an end-on bomber attack. By 1944, one hundred and sixty of the sites were destroyed by mainly dive-bombing attacks, as the sites were so small and confined. Our defences were also anti-aircraft fire and attacks from aircraft that flew out to sea to intercept and destroy. On one occasion a pilot named Dixie Dean of No 616 Squadron flying a Meteor, having run out of ammunition, tipped the bomb over with his wingtip. The gyro controlling the flight of the V1 precessed and spun the flying bomb into the ground. This was the first success for the Meteor in action.

In the artist's collection

One of the most exciting periods of the war, August 1944. The German army that had driven everything before it to occupy Holland, Denmark, Norway and France, now turned away from the Allied forces that landed on D-Day, 6 June. Rocket-firing Typhoons took a heavy toll of the retreating German forces. 'The intervention of the tactical air forces, especially the rocket-firing Typhoons, was decisive' said General von Lüttwitz. The Typhoons did not have far to fly. The dusty airstrips were busy all the daylight hours. The aircraft took off in pairs, returning briefly to be rearmed and refuelled. Alongside the airstrip where I worked, a school blackboard mounted on an easel gave the score of German tanks, armoured vehicles, etc, in a deadly mounting score, several hundred a day. They were retreating as fast as they had advanced through France. One had the feeling that they would not be back again and, moreover, we would not stop at the Rhine. It brought to mind the well-known words of Nelson: 'It is warm work, and this day may be the last to any of us at a moment, but, mark you, I would not be elsewhere for thousands.'

In the artist's collection

TYPHOONS TAKING OFF
FROM A NORMANDY
AIRSTRIP

36in x 26in

FALAISE GAP, AUGUST
1944
40in x 30in

To me and many others who were there, it was the turning point of the war. This painting was begun before the smoke of battle had died down. The assault lasted for ten days and turned retreat into an utter rout. The aircraft took off in pairs averaging over one thousand sorties a day.

I went down to the battlefield with some of the pilots. The ground was littered with burned-out vehicles and armour. Strewn across the fields were those who sought to seek safety off the deeply-cut roads and some, unsuccessful, were caught nose-to-tail there. Tanks were blown off the road, armoured vehicles burned out. They grey-clad bodies of German soldiers were everywhere, some still in their vehicles, sprawled over the seats, others on the running boards staring up at the sky – they mingled with the horses, dead in the shafts of stolen carts. Orchards were choked with the burned-out vehicles and the bodies of those who had sought the cover of the trees, their faces blackened with flies while, over everything, hung the sweet sickly smell of death.

It had to be painted. The dust and smoke of battle would have prevented any photographer obtaining an overall picture. I had to omit a great deal of the unpaintable. When I showed this painting to my C-in-C he looked at it intently for a while and said, 'Not enough dead Germans.'

By courtesy of The Imperial War Museum, London

During the war, immediately after the landings in Normandy, we had a mobile headquarters at Amblie, which was set up in a depression bulldozed out of the sandy soil, for the enemy lines were less than a mile away. As the enemy retreated, a variety of sites became available, and this was one of the most comfortable, being removed from the noise and dust of the airstrip. There was always an advanced landing ground nearby. My painting shows an Air Observation Post Auster flying in. These aircraft were used primarily for the observation of fire, also communications. Austers were frequently employed to precede tanks, reporting back on any likely resistance or white flags.

By kind permission of The Society of British Aerospace Companies

HQ NORMANDY, 1944
30in x 22in

TYPHOONS AT DISPERSAL, NORMANDY, 1944

36in x 27in

When 83 Group first operated from the beach-head, its Sabre engines developed inexplicable faults, later diagnosed by Napier's experts as due to abrasion of their sleeve valves by Normandy dust sucked in by the air scoops. It was discovered that Calvados was the source of the crushed grit used in the manufacture of emery paper. The engineers soon produced a modification to the air intake to eliminate the problem.

Owned by the artist

About twenty-five kilometres east of Dieppe, our second move from the beach-head. The weather was fine and the farmers were harvesting. Maintenance went on in strict rotation but under improvised conditions, as can be seen by the rural surroundings.

This was painted in about two to three hours, a ready-made subject. The little mark on the canvas near the small aircraft flying was a gash made by a piece of shrapnel. I had no proper means of repairing it, so I glued a small patch on the back of the canvas, which has held perfectly for the past forty-seven years.

Owned by the artist

MUSTANG
MAINTENANCE,
NORMANDY, 1944

24-HOUR INSPECTION, NORMANDY, 1944
30in x 20in

This was Group Captain Peter Donkin's aircraft undergoing a 24-hour inspection in a canvas hangar in Normandy, 1944. I remember the painting was finished in a little over three hours one morning, no easel. I held the canvas on my knees while sitting on an ammunition box.

By kind permission of Air Commodore P.L. Donkin, CBE, DSO.

Spitfires of No 154 Squadron RAF escorting B25 bombers over Italy in 1944. The Spitfire in the foreground, WHT, is still flying. In 1990, the present owner, Mr David Pennell very generously donated a limited edition of 850 prints to the RAF Benevolent Fund.

The original painting was unveiled by HM Queen Elizabeth II on 6 April 1990.

By kind permission of David Pennell, Esq.

TOP COVER
3: .. x 25in

NORTH SEA ATTACK
36in x 25in

I am very fortunate to have as friends and near neighbours two great leaders of Coastal Command Beaufighter squadrons, Air Chief Marshal Sir Neil Wheeler and Wing Commander Tony Gadd, both of whom flew from North Coates, although at different periods. Squadron Leader Wheeler, ex-Cranwell as he was then, commanded No 236 Squadron. Neil Wheeler was a natural leader and, holding firm views on a wing attack on an enemy convoy, introduced new theories and tactical training. This proved to be one of the most successful attacks the Wing had made and a significant defeat for the Germans.

Wing Commander Tony Gadd had flown with the Aircraft Torpedo Development Unit at Gosport and had dropped the amazing total of one thousand torpedoes on trial. He was Wing Commander Flying, North Coates, and led his squadron on several occasions against enemy shipping. He was awarded the DSO and DFC.

The illustration shows an attack on a German convoy made by the North Coates and Langham Strike Wings on 15 June 1944. Three ships, the *Amerskerk, M103* and *Nachtigall*, were destroyed and six damaged.

By kind permission of John S. Grace, Esq.

A role of great significance played by Coastal Command in this area of conflict. The attacks were mainly against German shipping bringing high-grade Swedish iron ore, the richest and least adulterated of all, from the ice-free port of Narvik in Norway across the North Sea to Rotterdam in Holland. The German coastal convoys were protected by 'flak ships' of about 500 tons, called 'Vorpostenboot', but there were also larger and more feared versions, called the 'Sperrbrecher' or 'Barrier-Breaker', usually ex-merchant vessels of up to 8,000 tons. These flak ships were packed with anti-aircraft guns, sometimes as many as seventy-two per ship.

The attack I have illustrated took place on 21 July 1944 off the East Friesian Islands. It shows a Beaufighter flown by Philip Brett of No 144 Squadron. He has just dropped a torpedo from a height of about 150ft, while one of the other aircraft from his Wing is attacking another ship with rockets. Two ships were sunk, others damaged and all the aircraft returned safely.

By kind permission of Brian Yeowart, Esq.

THE STRIKE WINGS
36in x 25in

B17 Flying Fortress

A frequent sight following the American daylight raids on Germany: a crippled B17 limping home late in the day, hoping to reach its airfield before dark.

The sun has set, but the last rays of sunlight give the decaying cumulus cloud a warm glow before nightfall.

Retraction Test, Salbani, India, 1945

Just after the painting was completed, a tropical dust storm blew a three-ton truck into the side of the Liberator causing extensive damage. I lost much of my painting gear. Luckily the picture was recovered a great distance away from where I was working and, because I was using 100-octane petrol as a medium which dried almost immediately, the painting did not collect an impasta of sand.

Presented to the RAF Museum by the artist

"ENGINE CHANGE" LIBERATOR 355 SQDN.
SALBANI INDIA
1945

WOOTTON

In many ways the Burma Campaign was handicapped by a number of shortages, very apparent to the officers and men facing the Japanese Army. At Salbani, situated on the flat desert plains one hundred miles north-west of Calcutta, two bomber squadrons, Nos 355 and 356 were based. It is evident here that the ground engineers were short of the normal equipment. An engine change is being carried out without proper hoists and engine cradles. The ground outside was sandy desert, not the best environment for carrying out aircraft engine maintenance.

At dispersal, it was found necessary to build sun pens to shelter the metal aircraft from the sun which raised the temperature of the exposed metal to dangerous levels, causing severe burns.

Presented to the RAF Museum by the artist

77

In the absence of cradles, the Liberator's Pratt and Whitney engine had to be lowered onto two blocks of timber covered with canvas to protect it from the sand.

Equipment often proved inadequate in the Far East, and it says a lot for the skill of the ground crews in overcoming the disadvantages. To keep the aircaft flying with such limitations was a truly magnificent feat. It should be remembered that, apart from shortcomings with certain equipment, the temperature ranged from 100°F upwards. The versatility and determination of the ground crews, with their consistently high morale, to endure hardship and discomfort while maintaining a high degree of serviceability contributed greatly to the success in the air.

By courtesy of The Imperial War Museum

LIBERATORS OF NO 356 SQUADRON BOMBING JAPANESE SUPPLY LINES, 1945
20in x 15in

No 184 Wing Liberators of No 356 Squadron bombing Japanese supply lines in the very steep wooded Chin Hills, averaging one thousand feet high. With the monsoon at its height, in turbulent air and torrential rain, the aircraft sought to cut at long range the enemy's supply routes in Burma, to destroy his dumps and sever communications. The squadron played a large part in overthrowing the Japanese, and after the fire and fury of the battle they bore food, clothes and medicines to sick and starving British prisoners of war. Finally, living up to their name, the Liberators flew the unconquered home.

By kind permission of the Royal Air Force College, Cranwell

MONSOON WEATHER IN BURMA
20in x 15in

The worst flying conditions in the world. The cumulo-nimbus clouds, cladding the hills, reaching 30,000ft and stretching for many miles in breadth, were at their worst in June-July. Many aircraft were lost in such extreme conditions. Flying beneath was often impossible due to the cloud base being lower than the mountain peaks. Further, load considerations and fuel could preclude flying above the clouds prevalent five months in the year.

In August 1944, a Spitfire squadron flying to Calcutta entered cumulo-nimbus cloud. Soon all the aircraft were beyond control, one being thrown from 5,000ft to 11,000ft and others forced down into the hills and lost. Four pilots took to their parachutes. The commanding officer was among the dead. Only eight arrived at their destination with hands cut to pieces in their efforts to control their aircraft. Of the pilots who crashed in the jungle, few survived.

By kind permission of the Royal Air Force College, Cranwell

**FIELD KITCHEN,
AIRMEN'S MESS,
SALBANI, INDIA**

As the airmen left the dining room, they would wash their plates and cutlery in hot water from this field kitchen. Usually they kept any scraps of meat left on their plates covered by another plate for, perched on the thatched roof, were always a fair number of predatory kitehawks. These birds would without fail swoop silently down behind the airmen and snatch any exposed piece of meat. The unremitting efforts of the men endeavouring to outwit the birds usually failed but, observing the maxim, 'If you can't beat them, join them', two airmen left the mess together with a piece of meat on each plate firmly tied together with a piece of string. The ensuing aerobatics resembled a World War I dogfight.

By courtesy of the Director of Catering, RAF Stanmore

Painted from the balcony surrounding the wooden control tower. This was always a busy airfield, the centre of communications in central Burma. Evidence of the long struggle with the Japanese to gain control of it is seen by the wrecked Dakota towed off the runway in the far distance, one of eight or more lost in the battle by the RAF, which was finally won with the aid of four hundred men of the RAF Regiment. Nearby was a large lake filled with the corpses of Japanese soldiers.

Notwithstanding, I found Meiktila a delightful place. In fact, when signalled by SEAC to fly to Kandy in Ceylon after VJ Day, I felt extremely disappointed at the thought of leaving. Aware of this, the commanding officer remarked gently that these signals directed to remote places in the Burmese jungle often took weeks to arrive. I thanked him and stayed a further fortnight.

Presented to the Royal Air Force Museum by the artist

MEIKTILA, BURMA, 1945   The capture of Meiktila at the end of February was the key to victory.

Kimura, the Japanese commander, constantly attacked the airfield. All our aircraft were targets for his guns. We lost seven Dakotas on 29 March. The RAF Regiment drove back two companies of Japanese, inflicting a loss of forty-eight killed. The regiment's own casualties numbered seven. Supplies were maintained by parachute. Finally, it was April when landings became possible again.

By kind permission of Peter Livanos, Esq.

No 607 Squadron Spitfires at Mingladon, Rangoon, Burma

Painted during the monsoon period in 1945, the airfield a sea of red mud with eight inches of water on the runway, deep enough to cause a Spitfire to nose over on landing and damage its propellor or the reduction gear.

You will see from the photograph that the aircraft I was painting has been towed away during the lunch break and another substituted. Judging from the remarks of the ground crew pointing out that I was looking at an A Squadron aircraft but had painted a B Squadron Spitfire, I knew that they hoped I would alter my painting.

SEAC aircraft colours were modified to eliminate the red on the roundel and fin to avoid confusion with the Japanese red spot.

Few fighter squadrons of the Royal Air Force in World War II can claim to have seen action in such widely differing climates as No 607 (County of Durham) Squadron, Royal Auxiliary Air Force. This squadron fought in France in May 1940, in the Battle of Britain, and finally in India and Burma.

In the artist's collection

PHOTO RECONNAISSANCE MOSQUITO OVERSHOOT

A victim of a short runway and difficult flying conditions during the monsoon period. Both the aircrew walked away. A sad end to a splendid aircraft, which was a great favourite of mine, for I was privileged to fly with Geoffrey de Havilland while testing the Mosquito, during my attachment to the de Havilland Company from the RAF in 1942.

Presented to the Royal Air Force Museum, by the artist

The aircraft is a Vickers Valetta C1 of No 48 Squadron, RAF Far East Transport Wing. Many free-fall supply drops were made to forts situated in the jungle of Malaya during the 1950s. It was essential to release the supplies from extremely low altitude, between fifty and one hundred feet for accuracy and to avoid undue damage to the packs on impact.

By kind permission of Air Commodore J.E. Bore, OBE.

THE AIRSPEED AMBASSADOR

A beautiful aircraft. I recall the day I was invited to Christchurch to paint it. I found the Chief Test Pilot, George Errington, working on his Bentley sports car. As I approached he said, 'I am sorry, Frank, but it has been badly bent. Ron Clear dropped it yesterday.' He took me around the corner of the hangar and there was the aircraft, down on its flattened belly minus its engines. George explained that Ron Clear was endeavouring to achieve a short landing distance when making his approach and had to cross the threshold at an altitude of 50ft, twenty per cent above the stall speed and with the aircraft loaded with the centre of gravity at its most forward position. Unfortunately, the approach was too steep or the speed too low and the aircraft failed to flare out, continuing downwards. The undercarriage was pushed up through the wing and the engines fell out. The aircraft bounced up *sans* engines, *sans* undercarriage. Fortunately, Ron was a competent glider pilot and was able to get it down without much further damage.

THE de HAVILLAND COMET 4C, NO 216 SQUADRON, TAKING OFF FROM KAI TAK, HONG KONG, 1960

Painted for the VIP room at Lyneham. The RAF flew me to Hong Kong to make this painting. A new runway had been constructed to take the larger and faster aircraft. Previously I had landed at Kai Tak, bordered on three sides by mountainous hills which, when covered with cloud down to two hundred feet, makes for a very hairy landing.

When the Comet first appeared, there was no counterpart flying. It was the first of its kind, the world's most advanced passenger aircraft. I was fortunate to fly in the Comet while taking part in some early test flights with Group Captain John Cunningham in 1950-51. It could fly higher and reach a higher Mach Number than the Meteor, the jet fighter of the RAF at the time. There was no restriction on where you could fly above 20,000ft, and no air traffic control.

I remember on one flight leaving Hatfield while Meteors based on Thorney Island were to carry out a practice interception. By the time we reached the coast, the Meteors were several thousand feet below the Comet, unable to intercept as they were then at the limit of their endurance.

By kind permission of RAF Lyneham

On my return from Singapore, I spent a week or so on the island of Gan. This was a staging post for the RAF. The runway was built on a small atoll and ran from one end of the island to the other. On the left can be seen the admin quarters. Swimming in the lagoon was the best I have ever experienced; palm trees leaning over the white sand and a complete absence of tourists. By arrangement, a number of Maldivians would either row or sail over from a nearby atoll each morning to work in the admin wing.

To obtain this view, I flew several circuits of the island in the bomb aimer's position of a Shackleton, sketching the scene each time round as the aircraft lined up with the runway.

*By kind permission of Air Chief Marshal
Sir Neil Wheeler, GCB, CBE, DSO, DFC, AFC.*

LIGHTNINGS OF NO 56 SQUADRON,
RAF WATTISHAM, 1965

60in x 40in

Of course, you can't go wrong. With the RAF behind you with all
the co-operation it can give an artist, it was a ready-made subject.
Mind you, it helps if you know what's going on.

By kind permission of Strike Command

Almost a prophetic record of the Vulcan painted before its last urgent wartime commission. Indeed, it was conceived and painted before the Falklands War, as the mighty delta-wing strategic bomber was about to be withdrawn from service with the RAF.

By courtesy of the Royal Air Force Club

THE LAST SCRAMBLE, 1982
36in x 25in

Painted while staying as a guest at Air House, Gibraltar, in April 1982. The Buccaneers were engaged on an exercise with naval forces in the Mediterranean.

The nearest point of the runway is only 550yds from the sheer face of the Rock. This can create intense turbulence, as the runway lies roughly east to west and is severely affected by crosswinds, which create difficulties for certain types of aircraft.

To reach the top of the Rock, 1,367ft above the airfield, involves a twenty-minute climb in a Land Rover; a very hairy experience. Only highly-qualified drivers are permitted to make this journey.

By kind permission of Alan Etherington, Esq.

The Lynx team gave a brilliant display of flying in different for-
mations, reminiscent of the manœuvres carried out by the Red
Arrows. I chose to paint this formation as it was one that the Red
Arrows could not perform.

*Presented to the Officers' Mess, Army Air Corps, Middle Wallop, by
Victor Gauntlett, Esq.*

Helicopter and tanks on an exercise.

Presented to the Museum of Army Flying, Middle Wallop, by the artist

The dogs are first trained to enter the helicopter with the rotors stationary, then, after familiarisation, are led in while the rotors are turning slowly.

Their task primarily is to patrol the border fences with China to deter illegal immigrants from crossing the border. Frequently the same immigrants are caught and returned to the Chinese side.

In the artist's collection

GURKHA SOLDIERS TRAINING DOGS TO ENTER A HELICOPTER AT SEK KONG, 1982

G. HAWK
30in x 20in

Painted for Sir Austin Pearce, chairman of British Aerospace and commissioned by his wife, Lady Pearce.

While chairman of British Aerospace, Sir Austin flew over Sussex in G. Hawk.

By kind permission of Sir Austin Pearce, CBE.

DESCENT TO INNSBRUCK
36in x 25in

Inspired by flights into the Tyrol along a very scenic route that crosses the Karwendel Gebirge. The wings of the aircraft appear to brush the Grösser Solstein (2542m), an illusion of course, due to the clear atmosphere in that region. In summer or winter, one of the most exciting scheduled flights.

By kind permission of The Society of British Aerospace Companies Limited

A unique and lovely aircraft designed for supersonic flight way way above the weather.

I have made four transatlantic flights in Concorde. Although I have appreciated the speed, the ultimate luxury of flying supersonic, I admit that I did feel a tinge of disappointment at each flight, simply because for me, as an artist, the greatest excitement when flying is climbing up through the clouds or descending through them so, naturally, I chose the latter for my painting.

By kind permission of Alan Etherington, Esq.

INDEX